# LIVING WITH
# LEUKEMIA

## Patsy Westcott

RSVP
RAINTREE
STECK-VAUGHN
PUBLISHERS
A Steck-Vaughn Company

Austin, Texas
www.steck-vaughn.com

## Titles in the series

| | |
|---|---|
| Living with Asthma | Living with Diabetes |
| Living with Blindness | Living with Down Syndrome |
| Living with Cerebral Palsy | Living with Epilepsy |
| Living with Deafness | Living with Leukemia |

Published by Raintree Steck-Vaughn Publishers, an imprint of Steck-Vaughn Company

Library of Congress Cataloging-in-Publication Data
Westcott, Patsy.
Living with leukemia / Patsy Westcott.
    p.    cm.—(Living with)
    Includes bibliographical references and index.
    Summary: Describes the condition of leukemia, how it affects the lives of those who have it, and how to cope with or recover from it..
    ISBN 0-8172-5743-8
    1. Leukemia—Juvenile literature.
    2. Leukemia in children—Juvenile literature.
    [1. Leukemia. 2. Diseases.]
    I. Title. II. Title: Leukemia
    RC643.W48 1999
    362.1'9699419—dc21          99-27219

Printed in Italy. Bound in the United States.
1 2 3 4 5 6 7 8 9 0 03 02 01 00 99

Picture acknowledgments
The publishers would like to thank Angela Hampton 11; Science Photo Library/Dr. Tony Brain 19 (left), /John Durham 19 (right), /Simon Fraser, Royal Victoria Infirmary, Newcastle 16, /Will & Deni MacIntyre 10, /Ed Young 14 (top); Tony Stone/Zigy Kaluzny *cover* (inset top), 18; Wayland photo library 8, 9. The remaining photographs were taken by Martyn F. Chillmaid.
The illustrations on pages 6 and 7 are by Michael Courtney.
Most of the people who have been photographed for this book are models.

# Contents

# Meet Susie, Jack, and Rosie

Susie is 14 years old. When Susie was 12, she had leukemia, a type of cancer. Susie's leukemia is in remission, which means that there are no more cancer cells in her blood. She has to go to the hospital for regular checkups to make sure the leukemia cells are not coming back. Susie's favorite school subject is art. She is very good at drawing and painting. When Susie leaves school, she would like to go to college to study art. In her spare time, she likes in-line skating and listening to music.

▷ After having treatment, Susie was able to do all the activities she likes again, such as skating.

▷ Jack wants to be a soccer player, when he grows older.

Jack is 10 years old. He lives with his parents and his brother, Tim, who is 8 years old. When Jack was 9, he developed leukemia and had to have treatment in the hospital. The hospital was a long way from where Jack lives, so his mother and Tim came and stayed in a house nearby. Jack and Tim went to the hospital school. Jack is at home again now that his leukemia is in remission, and he and Tim are back at their normal school. Jack likes playing with yo-yos, playing games on his computer, and playing soccer with Tim. Jack and Tim want to be soccer players when they grow up.

Rosie is 5 years old and has just started school. She lives with her parents, her brother, Jake, who is 8, and her sister, Chloe, who is 3. The doctor has just discovered that Rosie has leukemia. She is being treated in a hospital. Rosie likes to do ballet and play with her cat, Leo.

◁ Rosie and her cat, Leo, before she went into the hospital.

# What Is Leukemia?

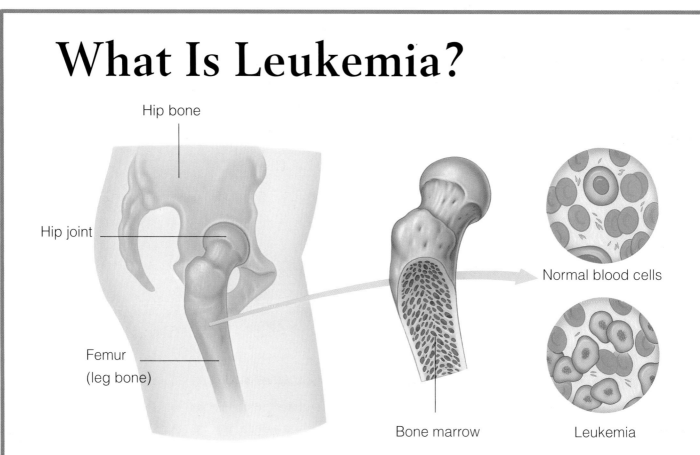

Hip bone

Hip joint

Femur
(leg bone)

Bone marrow

Normal blood cells

Leukemia

Leukemia is a type of cancer, an illness that happens when the cells in one part of the body start growing and dividing faster than normal. Doctors describe these abnormal cells as "malignant." If they are not treated, they can spread to other parts of the body.

Cancer can affect any part of the body. When cancer affects a solid body tissue, such as the muscles, the brain, or the kidneys, the cancer cells stick together and form a lump called a tumor. Leukemia is a cancer of the blood and the bone marrow, the soft, spongy material in the middle of the bones. The bone marrow is like a "factory" where new blood cells are made.

△ This illustration shows the difference between bone marrow with leukemic cells and with normal blood cells. Leukemia means more white blood cells and fewer platelets in the blood.

In leukemia, there are more white blood cells in the bone marrow than there should be, and they are not fully developed like normal white blood cells. These leukemic cells, as they are called, do not form a lump. Instead, they crowd the bone marrow and float around in the bloodstream.

**Types of blood cell**

The bone marrow makes three types of blood cells:
- red blood cells carry oxygen around your body;
- white blood cells fight the germs that cause coughs, colds, and other infections;
- platelets help your blood clot and prevent bleeding and bruising when you are injured.

When someone has leukemia, the white leukemic cells crowd out red cells and platelets, and the bone marrow is unable to make as many new cells as before.

▽ These are the different types of blood cells in your body.

Red blood cells

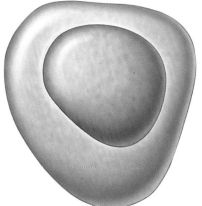

White blood cell

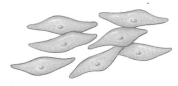

Platelets

## Types of leukemia

There are many different types of leukemia. Rosie has acute leukemia, and Jack and Susie had this type of leukemia, too. "Acute" is a word doctors use to describe an illness or a symptom that develops suddenly and progresses quickly. Both adults and children can develop leukemia, but acute leukemia is most common in children.

▽ Adults can get leukemia, but they don't usually have the same type as children get.

Many people feel frightened when they hear the word "leukemia" because thirty years ago most children who had the illness used to die. Leukemia is a very serious illness if it is not treated. However, there are medicines available today that are very successful in treating the disease, and many children with acute leukemia get better. In fact, seven out of ten children with leukemia are completely cured. Unfortunately, some types of leukemia are still hard to cure so, sadly, despite being treated, a few children do not get better.

△ The most common age for children to develop leukemia is between two and five years old.

# Why Do Some People Develop Leukemia?

▽ This woman is having an ultrasound scan to check the health of her baby. Leukemia may begin when a baby is still in its mother's womb.

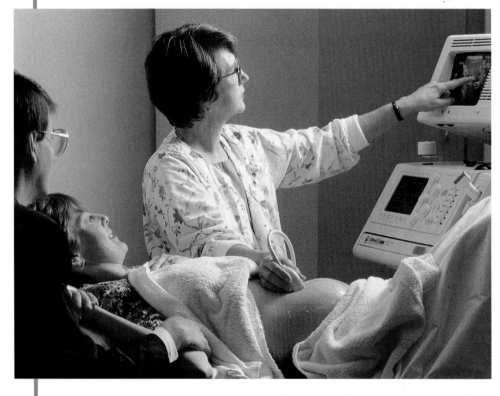

The exact causes of leukemia are not known. Acute leukemia starts with a mistake in a single white cell. This mistake gets copied over and over again as the cell divides, until there are billions of leukemic cells in the bone marrow and the blood. It is a bit like a spelling mistake in a story that is copied many times. Every time the story is copied, the mistake is repeated until there are a lot of copies, all with the same mistake.

Scientists are trying to find out why the mistake, called a mutation, happens in the cell in the first place. They have many different ideas. Some think that an infection or a virus causes some children to develop a rare reaction that causes the cell to change. Some think that the cell becomes damaged if a baby is exposed to X rays or certain chemicals while he or she is still in the womb or after birth.

Some scientists are trying to find out whether being exposed to electromagnetic fields from overhead electric power lines, and from substations where electricity is made, might cause damage to the cell. Others are studying the part that may be played by the genes, the material in your cells that governs the way your body behaves. When scientists discover what causes leukemia, other scientists will be able to design even better drugs and other treatments to help cure it.

Despite all this research, no one really knows what causes leukemia. However, we do know that you cannot catch it from someone who has got it, you cannot give it to someone else if you have it, and it is not caused by anything someone with leukemia has said or done.

△ Leukemia may be a disease that is passed on through a family's genes.

# What Are the Symptoms of Leukemia?

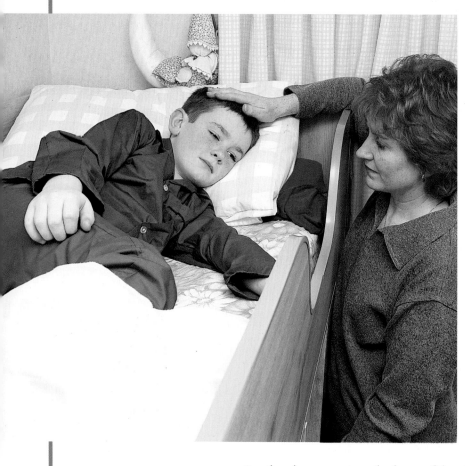

△ Leukemia made Jack feel tired and weak.

Jack always felt sick. He kept getting infections, such as colds, coughs, or sore throats, one after the other. Jack also felt tired a lot. When he got home from school, Jack would go straight up to his bedroom and lie down. He told his mother he felt limp and complained of pains in his arms and legs. He didn't like walking to school anymore because his legs ached so much.

One day, Jack noticed blood on his toothbrush when he cleaned his teeth. He told his mother. Jack also noticed that if he bumped into something, a big bruise would show up on his skin. His mother thought he looked pale and ill. Jack was fed up because he felt sick all the time.

The illnesses Jack experienced are typical of leukemia. However, there is no reason to think you have leukemia if you sometimes feel tired or get a cold or a bruise.

There are two reasons why leukemia causes these symptoms. First, the leukemic cells are dividing so fast that they crowd the bone marrow "factory," making it impossible for it to make the right amount of normal blood cells. Second, the leukemic cells travel in the blood to other parts of the body and keep them from working properly.

People with leukemia feel tired and weak because their bone marrow is making too few red blood cells. This results in a condition called anemia, which causes tiredness, breathlessness, and pale skin.

Pain in the bones is caused by the bone marrow becoming crowded with leukemic cells. Bruising and bleeding (for example, the bleeding from the gums that Jack noticed) happen because the bone marrow cannot make enough platelets.

The frequent infections people get when they have leukemia happen because there are not enough healthy white blood cells.

▽ Jack felt so tired that he didn't even want to play sports with his brother.

# Rosie's Tests

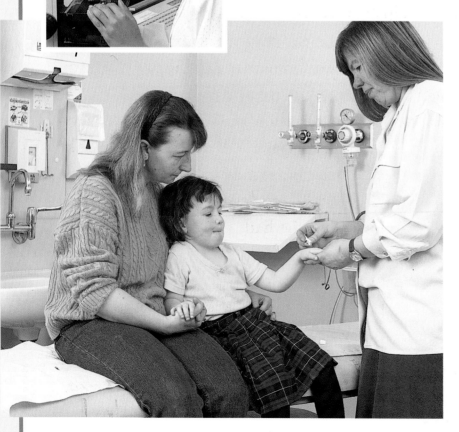

▽ Scientists can look closely at someone's blood cells through a microscope.

Rosie's mom was worried about Rosie's health, so she took her to the doctor. The doctor did some tests to try to help her find out what was wrong with Rosie. She used a needle to prick the back of Rosie's hand and draw out a small amount of blood. It didn't hurt because she put a special cream on Rosie's skin to keep her from feeling the prick.

Rosie's blood sample was sent to a hospital laboratory. A machine was used to count the numbers of white cells, red cells, and platelets in Rosie's blood. This is called a blood count. Some of Rosie's blood was put on a glass slide, and a scientist looked at it through a microscope. The scientist looking at Rosie's blood could tell she had leukemia because he saw a lot of unhealthy white cells and too few red cells and platelets.

◁ The doctor took a sample of Rosie's blood so a scientist could examine it.

▷ Rosie's doctor came to the house to tell her parents that Rosie had leukemia.

Another test used to diagnose leukemia is called a bone marrow biopsy. This test is done by drawing a small amount of bone marrow from inside the hip bone with a hollow needle. Before Rosie had her bone marrow biopsy, a doctor injected a special medicine called an anesthetic. The injection made her go to sleep for a while and kept her from feeling any pain. When the doctor looked at Rosie's bone marrow under the microscope, he could tell what type of leukemia she had.

When the hospital told Rosie's doctor that she had leukemia, she went to Rosie's house and told her mother and father. Rosie and her parents went straight to the hospital with the doctor.

## My tests

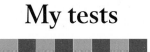

"When the doctor said she was going to do some tests, I felt a bit scared. She was really nice and told me that they would help find out why I was ill. They gave me medicines so I wouldn't hurt during the tests, so I really didn't need to be scared."

# Treating Leukemia

Jack, Susie, and Rosie had to take special drugs to kill the leukemic cells in their blood and bone marrow. This treatment is called chemotherapy. Several drugs are usually used to make sure all the leukemic cells are killed. Drugs can be taken by mouth as pills, but they are usually injected or given through a drip, a bag of medicine that can be pumped straight into the bloodstream through a special tube.

▽ This boy with leukemia is being given medicine through a drip. Chemotherapy treatment has caused his hair to fall out.

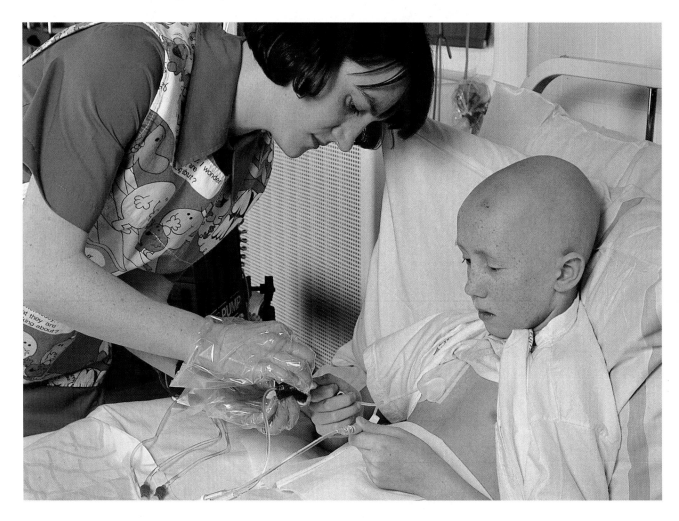

▷ Even though he has leukemia, Jack can still play soccer with his friends.

Often, a tube that goes straight into a vein is put into the chest or the groin. The proper name for this device is an intravenous line, although many children with leukemia may call it a "wiggly line." It is put in under an anesthetic, so the person does not feel anything. At the end of the line, a little tube pokes out of the skin with a rubber stopper on the end. When the doctors or nurses want to give the person drugs or take blood, they can use the line so the person does not have to have so many injections.

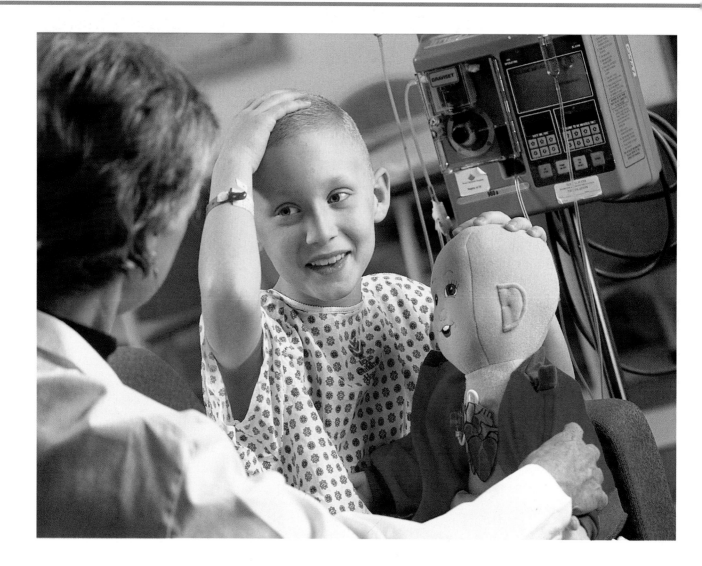

The drugs used to treat leukemia can sometimes make people feel sick. They may feel tired, get a funny taste in their mouth, and develop mouth ulcers or a sore stomach. Often their hair falls out. These side effects happen because the chemotherapy drugs do not kill only unhealthy leukemic cells. They also kill healthy cells such as those in the skin and the hair. Many side effects can be prevented. For example, a doctor can give people medicine to keep them from feeling sick. However, these side effects always go away once treatment is stopped.

△ This girl has lost her hair because of chemotherapy treatment. It will grow back again when the treatment is finished.

Sometimes radiotherapy is used. This treatment uses X rays to kill leukemic cells. After treatment has finished, the child may feel tired for a few days or weeks.

Often, treatments such as chemotherapy and radiotherapy make the leukemia go into remission. Sometimes the leukemia goes away but then comes back again. This is called relapsing. If someone relapses, he or she can sometimes have a bone marrow transplant. This replaces the unhealthy bone marrow cells with healthy ones. The healthy cells are taken from the bone marrow of a relative or someone else with cells that match those of the person with leukemia. This person is called a bone marrow donor.

▽ When seen under a microscope, the blood of someone with leukemia has a large number of abnormal white blood cells.

Healthy cells

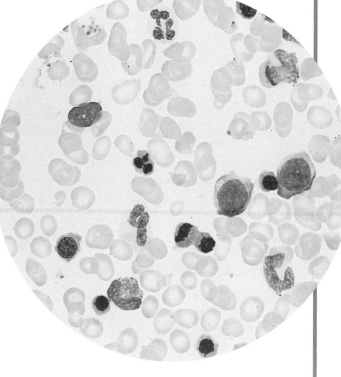

Leukemic cells

# Rosie Goes to the Hospital

Rosie has to stay in the hospital while she has chemotherapy. The hospital has nurses and doctors who are experienced in treating children with cancer. The hospital is in a different town from the one where she normally lives with her family, so Rosie's mom is staying in the hospital with her. Her brother and sister, Jake and Chloe, are staying at home with their dad. He visits her as often as he can.

## In the hospital

"I don't mind being in the hospital too much because my mom is with me, too."

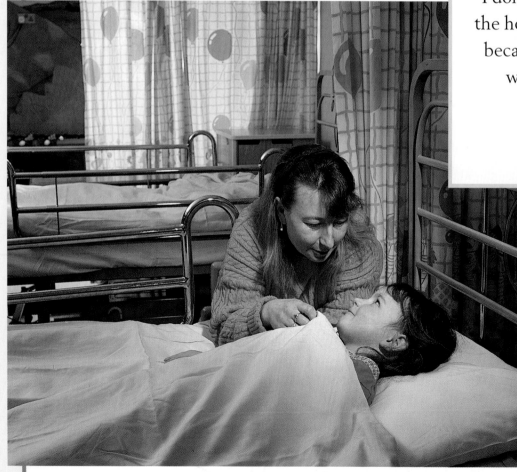

◁ Rosie's mother tucks her into bed every night at the hospital.

△ Rosie has a lot of toys to play with at the hospital.

In the hospital, Rosie has many toys to play with. Someone called a play therapist often comes and plays with her or reads her a story. On days when she feels a bit better, she goes to the hospital school. Rosie does not mind being away too much, but she misses her family and her cat, Leo.

Jake and Chloe miss Rosie, and they worry about her. Chloe draws a card and sends it to Rosie every day. Jake and Chloe do not like staying at home without their mother. They speak to her on the phone, and she comes back to see them, but sometimes she seems more worried about Rosie and spends most of the time talking to their grandmother. This makes Jake and Chloe angry, and sometimes they feel jealous of Rosie. They feel left out because people have bought Rosie a lot of presents. Sometimes they feel that people care more about Rosie than they do about them.

▷ Jake and Chloe like having their grandmother to look after them, but they miss having Rosie and their mother around.

# Jack and His Friends

Last year, Jack had to stay in the hospital, but now his leukemia is in remission, and he's back home. Jack has to have treatment for another two years to make sure the leukemic cells stay away for good. He has to go to the hospital for this, but he does not have to stay. Instead, he has his treatment in an out-patient clinic.

Sometimes after a treatment, Jack's white blood cell count is low. Then he has trouble fighting off infections like colds. If one of his friends has an infection when his blood count is low, Jack has to be careful to stay away. Jack's mother takes his temperature every day. If it is higher than normal, it could be a sign that he is developing an infection.

▽ Jack is happier now that his leukemia is in remission. Now he can play with his friends.

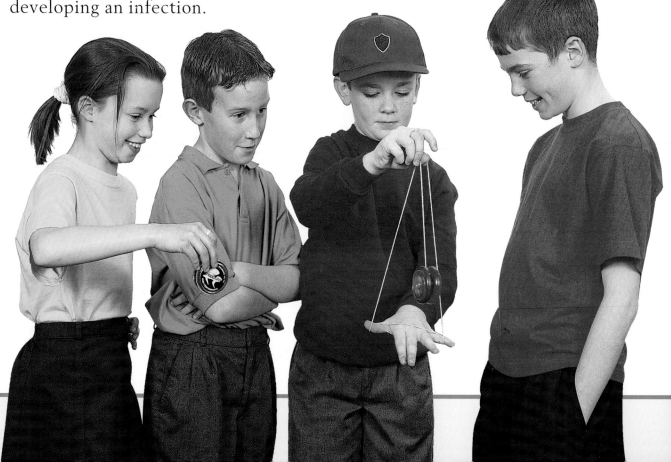

## Understanding leukemia

"Some of my friends kept away from me when I first came back. I think they felt embarrassed. When I talked to them about my leukemia, it helped them understand."

Jack has gone back to school. At first, he just went in the mornings, but as he began to feel stronger, he started staying all day. Sometimes, he feels tired and has to go home.

Jack was a bit worried about going back to school. He lost his hair while he was having chemotherapy, and sometimes he wears a hat. Although Jack's hair is growing back, he was worried that other children would stare or make fun of him.

Jack's friends are pleased that he's back home, but some of them felt embarrassed and did not know what to say to him. The community cancer nurse visited the school and told Jack's class all about leukemia. Jack told them about his leukemia, too, and showed them the end of his "wiggly line." Once Jack's friends understood about his leukemia, they did not feel embarrassed anymore.

# Susie Is Sad

Susie's leukemia is better now. She does not need to have any more treatment, but she still has to go to the hospital for checkups.

◁ Susie and her friend Emma spent many happy times together.

Susie belongs to a group for teenagers who have cancer or who used to have it. Her special friend at the group was a girl named Emma who had leukemia, too, but it was a different kind than Susie's leukemia. Susie and Emma enjoyed going shopping or seeing movies. Sometimes they slept over at each other's houses. One day, Emma told Susie that her leukemia had come back and she had to go back to the hospital for more treatment. Sadly, the treatment did not work. Emma's leukemia became so bad that she was not able to fight it anymore and she died.

Susie felt terrible when Emma died. She felt very sad and kept on crying. She was also frightened in case her leukemia came back, too, even though she knew it was a different type of leukemia than Emma's. Susie also felt angry that Emma had died. Sometimes, she felt angry with the doctors and nurses. Sometimes, she even felt angry with Emma.

Emma's mother invited Susie to come to Emma's funeral. Emma's family and many of her friends were there. Everybody was very sad, but after the funeral they all went back to Emma's house and talked about Emma. They remembered all the things Emma had done. Although Susie still feels sad, she also remembers all the good times they had together. She feels glad that she knew Emma.

## Being strong

"I think the fight against leukemia has made me stronger. If I can come through this, I can come through anything."

▷ Before Susie went home, Emma's mother gave Susie a necklace that belonged to Emma. Susie often wears it and thinks about her.

# Looking Toward the Future

Susie, Jack, and Rosie are just like you except that they have or have had leukemia. Apart from having treatment and sometimes having to stay in the hospital, their lives are just like yours. They still have fun with their friends, go to school, and enjoy having hobbies and doing all the kinds of things you and your friends like doing.

▽ Jack is glad to be back home with his family.

Jack, Susie, and Rosie know leukemia can be tough both for people who have the disease and for their friends and families. Treatment can sometimes cause side effects long after the cancer has gone away. Occasionally, children who have had leukemia have some problems with their memories. Sometimes, they may start to develop into adults later than other children, and sometimes when they grow up, they may not be able to have children of their own. The good news is that treatments are getting better all the time, and most children who have had leukemia will not have these problems.

△ Susie keeps in touch with other children and support groups all over the world by using the Internet.

Today, many children who have had leukemia can expect to grow up fit and healthy. They might go to college, have jobs, get married, and have families, just as you will. There are people who have had leukemia who have all sorts of jobs and live normal lives.

Jack, Susie, and Rosie are determined not to let leukemia beat them. They do not want you to feel sorry for them. They want you to understand and to recognize that they are still the same people they were before they developed leukemia so they can get on with their lives.

# Getting Help

△ Susie likes to talk about her experiences with leukemia with other children who have had the disease.

There are many organizations for children and adults who have leukemia or other forms of cancer. Most of them provide help, advice, and support for people with any kind of cancer. Others provide help and advice only on leukemia. Many hospitals provide books, videos, and other information or run their own support groups.

Some organizations are for adults and children with cancer. Others are just for children or teenagers. Many publish leaflets, books, and videos about cancer or leukemia. Some provide services like "homes from home" where children with cancer and their families can stay while they are having treatment. This service is especially helpful, because treatment may have to be done at a hospital far from their homes. Other organizations provide information on services in a particular town, city, or state.

**The Leukemia Society of America** is the largest private organization in the world that actively searches for cures for leukemia, lymphoma, Hodgkin's disease, and myeloma. The society also has many programs and services that aim to improve the quality of life for leukemia patients and their families. Among the Leukemia Society of America's services are the Patient Aid Program, which provides financial assistance to patients, and the Family Support Group, which brings together leukemia patients and their families to discuss their experiences with the disease. You can write to the Leukemia Society of America at 600 Third Avenue; New York, NY 10016, or call (212) 573-8484. You may also look at their web site at www.leukemia.org.

**Candlelighters Childhood Cancer Foundation** is the leading foundation in the field of pediatric cancer. Its mission is to educate, support, serve, and advocate for families of children of cancer, cancer survivors, and the professionals who care for them. Much of the foundation's work is done through the cooperation of parents and professionals. Candlelighters publishes newsletters and handbooks and oversees support groups nationwide. You can write to them at 7910 Woodmont Avenue, Suite 450; Bethesda, MD 20814, or call (800) 366-2223. You may visit their web site at www.candlelighters.org.

△ Most organizations hold fund-raising events to help fund resources and research into the treatment and causes of leukemia.

# Glossary

**Bloodstream** The movement of blood around your body.

**Bone marrow** The soft, spongy material in the center of your bones.

**Cells** Tiny parts of any living thing—plants, animals, or humans. Your skin, your hair, your nails, your blood, your bones, in fact all the parts of your body are made up of cells.

**Chemotherapy** Treatment with cancer-killing drugs.

**Clinic** Part of a building or a hospital where people go to have special treatment or advice.

**Diagnose** To work out what sort of disease someone has by looking at their symptoms and by carrying out tests.

**Electromagnetic field** Energy that is both electric and magnetic. This energy exists around electric cables containing a strong electric current.

**Infection** An illness that is passed from one person to another.

**Laboratory** A workshop where scientists do experiments.

**Malignant** Cells that have cancer. The cells are able to spread to other parts of the body.

**Platelets** Small blood cells that help the blood clot and prevent bleeding and bruising.

**Red blood cells** Cells that carry oxygen.

**Relapse** When the disease comes back after appearing to go away.

**Remission** When the abnormal cancer cells can no longer be seen in the blood.

**Side effects** Some effects of using a drug, which are usually unpleasant.

**Symptom** A sign that someone looks for to recognize an illness.

**Tissue** Parts of your body around your bones, such as muscle.

**Tumor** A swollen mass of diseased cells in body tissue.

**Vein** A part of the body through which blood moves.

**Virus** A possible cause of an infection.

**White blood cells** Blood cells that help the body fight off infections.

# Further information

**Books**

Gold, John Coopersmith. *Cancer* (Health Watch). New York: Crestwood House, 1997.

Kent, Deborah. *The Only Way Out*. New York: Scholastic (Apple), 1997.

Landau, Elaine. *Cancer* (Understanding Illness). New York: 21st Century Books, 1995.

Warner, Sally. *Sort of Forever*. New York: Knopf Books for Young Readers, 1998.

Gordon, Melanie Apel. *Let's Talk About When Kids Have Cancer*. Center City, MN: Hazelden Information Education, 1999.

Sanford, Doris. *No Longer Afraid: Living with Cancer*. Sisters, OR: Multnomah Publishers, 1992.

**Videos**

*Why, Charlie Brown, Why?* features well-known *Peanuts* characters to illustrate what happens when a friend develops leukemia. Available from the American Cancer Society and some hospital units.

**Web sites**

See suggestions on page 29.

# Index

Numbers in **bold** refer to pictures
as well as text.